waning

waning

Nué

Haymarket Books
Chicago, Illinois

Published in 2022 by
Haymarket Books
P.O. Box 180165
Chicago, IL 60618
773-583-7884
www.haymarketbooks.org
info@haymarketbooks.org

ISBN: 978-1-64259-850-6

Distributed to the trade in the US through Consortium Book Sales and Distribution (www.cbsd.com) and internationally through Ingram Publisher Services International (www.ingramcontent.com).

This book was published with the generous support of Lannan Foundation and Wallace Action Fund.

Special discounts are available for bulk purchases by organizations and institutions. Please call 773-583-7884 or email info@haymarketbooks.org for more information.

Cover artwork by Olivia Simone.

Printed in the United States.

Library of Congress Cataloging-in-Publication data is available.

10 9 8 7 6 5 4 3 2 1

For Nilah

contents

before leaving

The waning moon phase includes the last three phases of the lunar cycle. These are the phases in which the moon loses light rather than gaining it.

The waning phases begin the process of tapping into our intuition and going inward. These times focus on reflection, release, and recovery.

Embracing the darkness of the waning phases allows us to prepare for our following reset.

Waning Gibbous (reflection)
This is the time for reflection on what did or did not work for us. Showing gratitude overall is more important during this phase but especially for the earth, which can be done by giving back to it and offering more life. This is a good time to set things aflame, turning them to ash, releasing them from their physical form, and giving them back to the earth.

The Third Quarter (release)
This is the shortest phase, lasting only one day. This phase is for forgiveness, for yourself as well as others. It's important for any actions done in this phase to be done with forgiveness. This phase is for releasing all that no longer serves us, including burdens and obligations. The things that no longer serve us take up space we can use for welcoming new things that will serve us. The third quarter phase is the best time for self-care.

Waning Crescent (recovery)
This is the longest time in the waning period, lasting a full week. It is the longest period of darkness during the lunar cycle. The waning crescent marks the end of the entire lunar phase; this is the time for recovery. We should be least active during this period as this cycle calls for stillness and receiving.

Returning home

waning gibbous

I ain't sleep too well
so I'm going
        to sleep again until I get
it right
and on the train home I
goosebump over the idea
of a full-size bed being
the only thing to hold me
the way it does.
today I feel like
        don't hold my hand
    if you can't hold the rest of me.
today I feel like
        don't start something
        you can't finish.
tonight I feel like
        leaving
and not returning
until
I've rested
all the weary years
in eight hours of sleep.

Directions to find me

waning crescent

If you are looking for me and know it   or   *1*

I'll be a light in Chicago's cityscape or
a star in Mississippi's sky waiting
for you
I've been chasing my whole life
though
your papers are slow burners
        the lightness of your joint will
dissipate
the laughter of smoke sessions always grows old
into only echoes   bills get high as us
in the city   someone will have to flip the switch

Ain't you ever disappeared before?
We don't blend in with the blackness
we become it

                2   or   *If you are looking for me and don't know it*

Find the nearest blackness
Whether it's the ink you're reading, a pot of greens, an elbow, a turned-off
phone, the iris of a pea, a city's sky.
                                Then find yourself lost in it.
If you come for me, follow the music, let your knees unbuckle,
                put on the dirty sneakers in your trunk.
If you come for me, come with empty solo cups,
                bring a bib and a tongue ready for fingers.
I'm leaving tonight and you're either coming   after   or   with me.

    Stars always burn out   we all fade   I've been chasing my whole life.
Who will run for me?
    Hurry.

Reflections with my therapist

waning gibbous

After taking care of everything around me, I tell my therapist how empty I am. She asks for words but I gave my last few to a friend's friend a couple of hours ago.
She still asks questions.

I don't know what I want therapy for.

Do I want to work through things within myself? Or
do I want somebody that will listen to me with the only condition of them getting paid? Which is why I have to remind myself that she's not here for what I need love to be here for.
I just feel like therapy is taxing. Though I feel like she'll steer me in the right direction, I fear she will do so while pointing out more things I need to do while I'm working double shifts.

Revelations are so   tiring
when they topple atop of all the other work happening for survival purposes in a capitalist state.
I'm so used to giving everything I have to everyone
                                        and I'm so tired.
But if I don't have emotional space for myself, then who do I have it for (is what she asks me often)?

I would ask someone for help if I needed help; but I'm at the point where I'm sure someone can just do it for me and I wonder why that can't be her. She's there for me when I tell her I've been too busy to go searching for the love I've been needing to fall on my doormat.

Working on it

waning crescent

She doesn't answer my calls when she's at work
But I'm work   I'm work she can work on
I work 2 jobs and am working on a third   I got so much work if you
knew about it you'd take a piece to call your own
My mom tells me that I'm a piece of work
                but apparently, I'm the whole damn thing.
                I go to therapy for her to tell me I got work to do
                I tell her I'm on the market right now for someone
                    who can do that work for me
                she tells me it doesn't work like that
I got all this space and no one   to fill it up with   still working on that
feeling of needing someone to move my mind to the times before I was
working for survival
                cause the only thing that holds me
                back nowadays are year-old grudges
turns out I never took all the pocketed sunshine out of my jeans during
laundry
and lately all the sunsets have been soggy like crumpled-up love letters
thrown in the lake   I been working on my breast stroke to go get every-
thing I've ever wanted
                back
I've been working on loosening my grip on all the realities I made
when truth was
 but a teary-eyed nina song

I've been working on my patience
  still waiting for someone to come
 and work my body as the graveyard shift it is
                      Work themselves to death   For me
All I ask is for someone to do the labor of affirming me that this is
n't forever
My therapist asks how I've been and I tell her
busy
busy

busier

          I fired everyone
          who made more work for me instead
          of treating me like a job that
          fed them
This is a cry for someone to put their claim on me
          and just start working like they're on payroll and
          their temples sprout those beads of sweat that a hard
          worker would deem so affirming

When I become a seed and time turns to
 when I should be pressed down into the earth
 I want someone's claim on me like the ground can't just have one of us it
has to swallow us both

     Nu.   *My nigga, my round,*   *I miss ha.*

Broke boy blues

third quarter

                              bill
                             bills
                        bus [un]fare

i owe my shadow dinner and $15
for every time i disappeared and
it apologized for my absence

              i get too busy in sadness to remember
to call/text back

            dad thinks i'm only here
        because my phone will be off
        soon or that my bank balance
        growls the same songs as my stomach
                        i am here in his messages   to ask
                        how he's been   and to know if he still
                        has open arms

BIG

waning gibbous

Daddy has always been big
Big hands   so big they swallowed mines
        when we crossed the street
Big enough to hold my whole body
        and throw it over his big shoulders
He'd play basketball with the 40+ year olds
        at Grand Crossing playing with skinny 6 footers
His 5'9" always been big to me, especially when
        he stopped running and his belly grew
                into something he'd always introduce as something
                        he's "working on"
Big man always working on somebody's something
        If he isn't
        he's letting out big snores from remodeling
        kitchens or bathrooms
        If he isn't
        he's letting off big steam by swinging the club
        and unearthing a little grass
        If he isn't
        he's crying big storms cause his kid grew a little
        overnight without him knowing
        and they say shit like "shit" or "fuck" now
        If he isn't
        he's cooking big meals for small groups
        of small mouths
        If he isn't
        he's smiling at anything on VH1
        because their relationships make him feel
        better about his
        If he isn't
        he is trying to drill in my big head
        how much he loves me
He so big   he don't care about how
small he comes across

He so big he got a heart that resembles
a sixth of his weight
He so big his smile is as long

———————

My dad gets drunk for the hell of it

waning gibbous

and tells me how
out of all the women he's dated, he's only not cheated
on three. One of those women was my mom.
I know we both are too familiar with her.
He is silently sure she's cheated on him.

I've got her inconsiderate running in my blood
her bad habit of deleting messages.
How she constantly introduced ugly men to my younger brother
and I. They just get uglier and uglier and uglier making me think
she still misses something about my dad. She can't find one with my dad's
amount of personality.

His blotched black and pink lips
break up to touch on more crown royal. He says
    Your mother has said things to me,
    that if I was a man that hit women, I'd be scared

Reminds me of how sharp her teeth are
how I learned how to kill a man
without tiring my tongue.
His eyes crease in realization and says
  I don't think she knows how to love a man, really.

I think of when Glen bawled his eyes
out in the car on the way to buying us dinner.
He weeps and she asks him if he is still going to up money
for our school uniforms. Eugene has been in love with my mom since the
seventh grade.
She declines his calls twelve times in a day and he still
sends me $100 for my trip to New York.
My dad cries when I forget
    Sometimes it feels like you're using me.
Again, I forget to text back

until my phone bill is due and I'm reminded of another man
at the feet of another woman who doesn't know how to
close her eyes and kiss
his scruffy cheek.

Sorry ain't good enough

waning gibbous

First thing to crawl out of a jawed cave
is a damp pitiful sorry
Damn
in realization that there's nothing else
to sell someone who you have
questioning
if they can love again.
            She mentions how all that I have to offer are sorry's
she's got so many
they're spilling out of her ears—

                        Sorry is a sorry word
they just pile
ontop
of
eachother
until
        they form
                a mountain
                    of stilled issues
                        still   ain't worth a damn   can't buy a
                pack of advils for the
headaches that follow after.
So I look for another language to apologize in
I'm sorry—
I mean—   dogs aren't born bad, they are only
what they've been taught.
        I mean sometimes I forget to put these old teeth away.

I'm sorry   I always do this,
        apologizing for things I had no
participation in.
If given the opportunity
I would apologize for my mom

20

and dad having
the same computer science
class in college—

I rather pull teeth
than to give out another sorry
    to be sorry for later.

My friend says it's the Pisces in me.
I was born apologizing
for nothing & everything.
She tells me to stop
Scrape them from the roof of my mouth
I still got a few pickled sorries hidden
under my tongue—
She says I'll live so much
better without the grotty taste in my mouth.
She says open up   I do.
They're rotting my teeth
all that sugar   I'm too sweet. It's better
a sorry escaped first
than silence followed by a   *you're in my prayers*

                                         right?

There's nothing to give
to a mother who's been stripped of that title
                      I'm sorry to hear that
I mean,   if I could cry a river
to wash your baby back up
& breathing
I would. I mean   I'll still try.
I mean   sorry, that this is all the world has to offer you
        me   standing pigeon-toed
offering sorries like they're currency
        when I don't have any spare change
                but this poem.
Every time I tried to send a prayer up
they got stuck in space
and decided on just becoming stars
instead.

For me to forgive you

third quarter

I would need one of us to have never been born
or
for our paths to have crossed and we too focused on our destination
no time   even for eye contact
I would need
you to take up the hobby of magic and master the disappearance trick and
by master I mean   do it and do it again and do it again until that is
the only direction
you know how to move your body in
I would need
for you to have at least a little guilt sitting
                    in your stomach enough to make you get up
            and move
some   things   around
Tell me
                    your guilt ate before you did today
what you had to get off your chest was your chest
    your feelings are what a sorry could never amount to being
                    I've been practicing accepting
                    absences and apologies
                    of persons and their promises
                    with practice comes learning I for
                    get   Your shit
                    [isn't] together
                                    just as much as mines
            and learning   that not everything I want is as practical
or possible as I'd like it to be
But   still

                                    I'm still learning
                        we don't always have the space for ourselves
                            to make more of it   for others
                            so I surrender to as much as I can
                                                        Maybe
If you hadn't given me reason to bring fire to the bridge

22

my hands wouldn't have learned engineering
to build a crossing out of ashes

Compromise everything to
meet me in the middle of it

Maybe I'll forgive you
for nobody's sake but my own

Maybe

I do owe odes to our paths crossing

Some shit just has to be done   *Some shit just has to be let go*

Bad things don't last forever   (interlude)

waning crescent

We're taking space like I'm going to love her any less when we meet again.

Space sounds like no

phone calls.

Space is confusing; it's to fight off relationship

codependency.

We don't talk and I miss the me that is with her. I miss the honey stick of her lip

gloss. I miss her singing directly in my hair.

We take space when there is an issue but I want to take up the space that surrounds the issue

until it no longer exists.

We're taking space, but I want the space that surrounds her.

We aren't talking now and I want to take up all the space in the room.

The space I want to take up is the space in her rib cage. I want to live

there.

I'm working on being alone, being for me.

But right now, there's nothing else in this world that I want more than her right now. I love me in my space,

but ~~sometimes~~ I love her in it too.

Playing with fire

waning gibbous

don't you ever forget
that mark on your neck
is not the birthmark
or bad tan you tell people it is
it is the survival scar
from an umbilical cord

you have done the hard part already

you have survived   when you weren't supposed to
you were born
you inhaled   and savored
you know the feeling of being denied a throat
to be stuck inside of your peel
so thirsty to get out you didn't even notice
you couldn't swallow
you know the feeling
of being swallowed

you know there is always a way out   c section your way
out of a choking poverty
it will leave a scar
on your mother
and your neck   but scars make
for good stories

remember that time when you wondered why
it felt so nice when she choked you
and kissed you   afterward

or when you wondered
how long did it take until the last breath
was let out of a fruit   remember

discovering life by feeling how closely
it clung to death

don't you ever forget
there is always heaven after
each
and every
gasp.

Spring Cleaning

Even far far away
from home I still
am turning my head
at all times
like double-checking corners
I've already swept
I am convinced my
dad knows a third
of the city—
Or my mom's side of the family will spot
me coincidentally
who will my face be familiar to?
I am too paranoid
to be outside
with her hand in mines
and to not be out

Under a roof
we take advantage
of comfort
and remove our clothes
we are too busy loving each other
to hear the locks undo themselves

We are scrambling
like we overslept 3 alarms
we get everything that proves her
and her existence here
we shove them into my closet
and this is not the first time
It's actually routine
She makes a joke and says
It's cool, I know my place

I weep inside from being tired
of tiring lovers
stuffing them into a place
they were less coward
than me to escape

She says
when you're with me
you always worried
like you are scared
to be with me

I apologize for turning
her into a skeleton

When we are alive and around
my mom
we become best friends
        I know lights dim for her
She looks up to see hoodies and jeans hanging
looking like the bottom of dirty feet

I am sorry
for the girls I've turned
into bones
My closet is becoming full
and dry
of girl's dead tiredness
I hope to have the courage to become their alive self
Out
And I'm wondering
maybe I just need to stop having sex in my parents' home
when I don't know when they get off of work

Fucked up poem

after "Hands on Ya Knees" by Danez Smith

We try giving each other nicknames
and with every inch in her 5'0" stature
she calls me
Daddy long legs

And I know where this is going.
but I ask anyway

She answers
Because you're daddyish and tall

& I don't do this often
But when a girl I barely know calls me daddyish
I let her
As a matter of fact
for the first time ever
I become what she thought I already was

I stuff my womanhood in my pockets and let it sag my pants
Grab my groin
spread my legs when I sit
erect my chin
Clasp my hands together to form a cocoon
whenever they open again
out will crawl arachnids
with their long long legs
she said she likes my long long legs
I let the hair on them grow a long long time ago
Like my sideburns
long long as the paragraphs she sends me.

I only pop up on special occasions now
birthdays
National Honors Society Ceremony

When she asks to link
I grow a fear of chains
She says she wants to be with me
I tell her to go ask her mother

She keeps asking me
What are we?
Do you like me?
Are we friends?

She tells me about her boyfriend
I explain why she cannot have one of those
She asks me
who do I think I am
& I remind her
Daddy
I never asked to be put here
But she placed me in this position
I think to tell her I'm going on a trip
and ditch the responsibility of raising this relationship

When a girl I barely know calls me daddyish
instead of calling her weird
I just get even weirder
Instead of kissing her on the mouth
I'll kiss her forehead with ghost lips
She called me and I texted her back
who is this?
Our phone calls came to a halt
and I mason jar her voicemails
She questions my absence
and asks why I've gone deadbeat

How I describe her to others

waning gibbous

she so pretty
she reminds me of these calm waters
they so still
they still   look dead
they so dead   i know she couldn't be
afraid of them
she so pretty she looks
like the water
she's so scared of
she so pretty she look like
lilacs lying atop the lake
she look like the earth
she's trying so desperately to save

two mosquitoes died in some amber sap
and that's how her eyes happened
i'm still being sucked in
two halves of a big snowy mountain fell
out of love with each other
and that's how her teeth happened

jean baptiste point du sable called the land chicago
and that's how her heart started beating
she was delivered on the 115 bus   to me

Vs. What I Say to Her
I love you how I love this big ole city

With the big ole sky
dangling over crowned tops with its big ole sun
that places the dazzle on top of the wet rocks
on the shore of the lake but this time in the middle of your
eye. Today is a perfect day to love all of you
I've got as much time as there are clouds in my forehead

Has anyone ever told you   you are a dream?

              coming out the tunnel that you are the sunset
over Cermak? A sight so heavy a mirror couldn't hold it.
You're the skyline reflecting itself over the docks of Navy Pier.
Only the water could carry the weight of all that gorgeous.
All those lights. An entire ferris wheel
with all those seats like on the train on its way
to a bus going to your porch with roses in hand
to kiss your soft
soft
hands.

This is actually to all the girls I wrote poems to & they didn't deserve it!

third quarter

what's the difference between an empty page
and a full page of empty words?

i sat there and watched the ink turn
itself from a stain off of paper
during an attempt to unbuild
the cities i built for girls

the thing about writing is it is only
undone in fire
or water or twisting hands powered by a hot fury

i already exhausted energy writing
i need to flip the page and it not exist

when words don't feel truth in them
anymore, why don't they just dissipate
within themselves and the space
around them
like stars?   aren't poems stars anyway?

i meant it in the moment
i swear on a promise
i did
but you ain't all that sweet
like i thought you were

The prettiest girl in the world

third quarter

I want a confidence so BIG
I kiss the prettiest girl in the world
and make her blush the way no one has

I'd call her all type of sweet thangs
like
sweet thang!

I'd take her dancing
and she can't dance
but she just has to dance with me

The prettiest girl in the world just has to have a drink
with me or she'd cry
fall asleep in my arms
or she'd die

The prettiest girl in the world is going to go
in the bathroom to freshen up
for me   and when she looks up from the sink
I'll be the one she sees in the mirror   Lately
I've been the only thing on her mind

We'll go out for a movie
and people will look at me all types of crazy-
cause I'm laughing and I'm talking
to the prettiest girl in the world
We share popcorn and a box of goobers

Who knew her favorites
would be mines

The prettiest girl just wants
to be around me

with no outside interruptions
She can't even feel my kiss
only when i kiss the back of her hand

I'm the only one holding her hand

sweet thang
sweet sweet sweet sweet sweet

I'll be coming back

I left that rock to find the love
of my life and turns
out it's the moon after all   Everything

 we got in common only kills
all gravity

The moon asks about where I come from
Oh baby you got to come
down to Mississippi
nothing like space. It's so hot down there everything is fried
Moon says they ain't ever moving
not even gone think on it
     except for that one time I got us
an air bnb down south and my aunt
said we best not do that again
when she has an extra room that gets
as lonely as she does
     and we went to a family outing and ate whatever smoked
on the back of his truck.
Moon seen what I called home
and almost stuttered it the same thing
after looking up and seeing all those stars and saying

you must not know lonely here
and I reassure her
ain't no streetlights here

Ashy nigga

waning gibbous

Yeah my hands ashy.
                    So what?
I'm a ashy nigga. I once tried
to steal some lotion from the Target right across the street from my job

but they let me go cause
what you gone do to an ashy nigga the ash ain't already done?

There is nothing new under the sun
There is nothing new under this ashy moon
it's all just old aging soil
so I buy myself flowers
while I'm still alive. Pockets full
of posies
ashes ashes
we all fall someday
I'm just making sure it's not today.
Even with all the burning around me I'm still
chasing after the sun and everything
under it posing to be new

        I'm writing the best thing ever
written, I ain't thinking 'bout no lotion!
        I just ran after a bus that ran
from me, I ain't thinking 'bout no lotion!
        Why does my hands being moisturized matter if I'm holding
my grandma's,
        or if my love kisses them before moonlight,
        I got a bag holding product that's going to
put food in a pot tonight. I ain't thinking
'bout no lotion
        I worked all day and you think
I'm thinking 'bout some lotion?
        I washed my hands of 8 hours of work and bought my hands

some new ashy
I ain't thinking 'bout no
lotion
or no soft hands. Ain't nothing   soft
about this love!

Waning

third quarter

Are you really crying if no one is around to hear
or are you singing a song
in a different language?

I am trying to become friends with loneliness
but she hurt me so
badly it's hard not to hold
a grudge

I balled up and cried on my
living room rug and even it wouldn't
hold me back
    cried so loud
my throat turned
into a dim hallway

          There was no one
in the entire apartment complex
There was no one on the block
I cried myself into space and the soundwaves
traveled to move around a few stars
and altered orbits
I cried a retrograde
Now everyone is crying
But does it really matter
if I can't see them when they do?

Are you really crying if no one is around to hear?
Ain't no one around here
that's gone listen long enough to know
whether to rub your back or feed
the rumbling bellies in your ears only sweet things

I cry so big it covers everything small too

I moved molecules of matter
in a matter of minutes
I can turn water into peroxide
            turn water into witch hazel
            turn water into both kinds of alcohol
and no one knows
I got things going for me

Ain't it true that dogs
howl in hopes to finally find
understanding?
I howled at the moon
            it howled back
and we wept
about our loneliness together

Broke

third quarter

Leaving school early was easier
than saying *I don't
have it*, and been gas
lighted on fire for
>   *You don't have $25 for gas
>   for me to get to work?
>   For me to take you to the bus?*

Hopping on a train
then a bus and another
because I don't have it but
I have two last joints that once
made my fingertips
stick together now stick to another
green. Reminds me how it all comes
from the same dying rock
suffocating on gas to get me to
my bus to get to school.

I need school like
the earth needs me.

Without my last two joints in
the shiny small resealable
plastic bag
will I get gas
to get to school
to save the world?

Dee's palms inhale the two joints
and exhale $25
For travel.

The last bus stops running at 11

waning crescent

When the sun goes down we are speedy
snails, slugging our bodies, yearning for our feet
to unite with our porch steps. We leave a slimy trail of sweat that slips from
the creases of our foreheads that work gave us
With the droop of daytime comes the drip
of the corners of the bus driver's mouth
How his face sags down to the souls of his shoes
like jean back pockets that dwell behind knees
How denim dangles on the Dan Ryan's thighs like dreads
I think
the 115
Waits for me at 95th. faces   jeans   hair ambition
all sagging
gatheronthisbusinacluster and we are fall
ing fireworks
to sink further south into the city like mother's breast in a spaghetti strap
We are all floor huggers
weep like willows and wilt in Chicago's cool night heat
At 10 p.m. on the 115, it is finally okay for black folk to be dead white light
fallen stars onto earth's surface.

acknowledgments

Thank you, Haymarket, for all of your production and patience.

Thank you, E'mon, Jamila, and Dominique.
Thank you, Ana, a true lightbeam. Thank you, Naya. Thank you, Bank$.

Thank you, Nick. Thank you, Doug.

Thank you again, E'mon. Your patience and capacity knows no bounds.
Thank you, Olivia, for your talented hands and Jhori for your love.

Thank you, Grandma, for keeping me alive.
Thank you, Ashley, Cassandra, and Fredia, for showing me the truest form of family.
Thank you, Jackson, Mississippi, for loving me every day of every year and only seeing me once every 2.

Thank you, Nikki and Morgan, for pulling words out of me without ever meeting me.

Thank you, Phillip, for being amazing and perfect and making me think the same of myself.
Thank you, Crews.

Thank you to old lovers for being old lovers.

I could never forget your sweetness
or when you were there when I needed you most.

about the author

NUÉ FOSTER is a Blk queer artist from the far south side of Chicago where they call The Hundreds home. They were deemed Chicago's 2020 Youth Poet Laureate and have had their work featured on many reputable platforms such as The Aids Foundation Chicago, BBC Radio, and Nike. Their work has also been performed on the stages of the Pitchfork Music Festival, Windy City Live, Newberry Library, Driehaus Museum, WNDR Museum, and Young Chicago Authors' Louder Than a Bomb poetry festival in which they won in 2020 as an individual.

They were a two-time participant in the Bomb Squad internship and a current participant in YCA's Next Gen apprenticeship. Nué's poetry journeys through self-discovery in a coming-of-age fashion where accountability prohibits them from being centered as a hero in their stories. Their poetry is offered as an invitation to accompany them in interrogating their truths.

CPSIA information can be obtained
at www.ICGtesting.com
Printed in the USA
JSHW021019180422
24973JS00001B/1

9 781642 598506